SUPER SMART INFORMATION STRATEGIES

ONLINE ETIQUETTE AND SAFETY

by Phyllis Cornwall

CHERRY LAKE PUBLISHING • ANN ARBOR, MICHIGAN

A NOTE TO PARENTS AND TEACHERS: Please remind your children how to stay safe online before they do the activities in this book.

A NOTE TO KIDS: Always remember your safety comes first!

CHERRY LAKE Publishing

Published in the United States of America
by Cherry Lake Publishing
Ann Arbor, Michigan
www.cherrylakepublishing.com

Content Adviser: Gail Dickinson, PhD,
Associate Professor, Old Dominion University,
Norfolk, Virginia

Book design and illustration: The Design Lab

Photo credits: Cover, ©gsmad/Shutterstock, Inc.; page 4, ©iStockphoto.com/zorani; page 8, ©iStockphoto.com/aldomurillo; page 11, ©iStockphoto.com/fatihhoca; page 13, ©iStockphoto.com/kihoto; page 19, ©iStockphoto.com/skynesher; page 25, ©Elena Elisseeva/Shutterstock, Inc.; page 29, ©Yuri Arcurs/Shutterstock, Inc.

Library of Congress Cataloging-in-Publication Data
Cornwall, Phyllis.
Super smart information strategies. Online etiquette and safety/
by Phyllis Cornwall.
p. cm.—(Information explorer)
Includes bibliographical references and index.
ISBN-13: 978-1-60279-956-1 (lib. bdg.)
ISBN-13: 978-1-61080-260-4 (pbk.)
1. Online etiquette—Juvenile literature. 2. Internet—Safety measures—Juvenile literature. 3. Internet—Moral and ethical aspects—Juvenile literature. I. Title. II. Series.
TK5105.878.C67 2010 2010002023
004.67'8—dc22

Cherry Lake Publishing would like to acknowledge the work of The Partnership for 21st Century Skills. Please visit *www.21stcenturyskills.org* for more information.

Printed in the United States of America
Corporate Graphics Inc.
July 2011
CLFA09

Table of Contents

SAFETY FIRST

CHAPTER ONE

What Is Online Etiquette?

Do you practice good etiquette when walking through school hallways?

Do you know what etiquette is? Etiquette can be thought of as good manners and behavior. Some people call them social rules. Etiquette helps us choose proper behavior in different situations.

To understand etiquette, it helps to think about how your actions might affect others. Imagine going from your classroom to the gym with your classmates. You watch where you are going so you don't bump into anyone. You also stay quiet. That way, you don't disrupt other classes as you pass by. Suddenly, one of your classmates begins running and yelling, "I'm faster than everyone!" Then, the whole class takes off running. Soon, there is pushing, shoving, and yelling. Nobody wants to be the last one to the gym!

THERE ARE NO RULES

TRY THIS!

What would happen if people made up their own rules of behavior? Think of a favorite board game. Then find a friend or family member who doesn't know how to play it. Start playing without explaining the rules or purpose of the game. Is he or she asking you questions? Is the person confused? Now explain the rules and play again.

Don't things run more smoothly when everyone knows and follows the rules? The same is true with etiquette. If everyone follows some rules of courtesy, we can get along better.

What happens when people do not practice proper etiquette? In this case, children could have gotten hurt. Classes would have been distracted. Your teacher would have been upset. This example might seem silly. Your class never runs down the hall. See? You already follow hallway etiquette. You also have an idea of how following—or not following—the rules of etiquette can affect others.

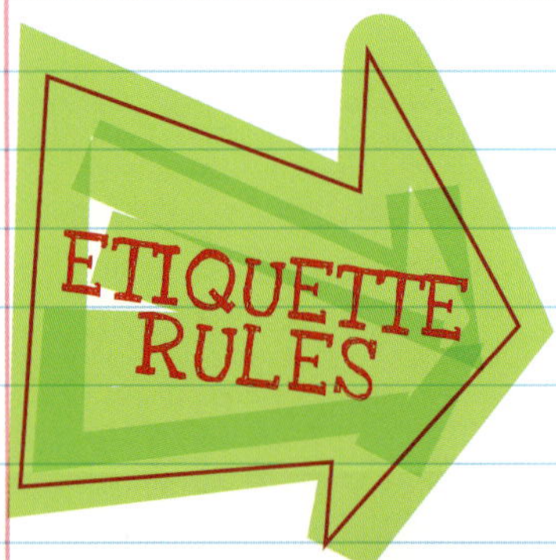

Sometimes, rules are clearly expressed on signs. A poster in a movie theater that says "Silence All Cell Phones" is one example. Etiquette may not be written. Instead, it is generally understood and followed. For example, most people know not to talk in a theater once the movie has started.

It is important to practice proper etiquette in our everyday world. The same is true in the online world. Online etiquette involves proper behavior for users of online services and the Internet. When you practice online etiquette, you are respectful of others. You also avoid bad behavior. One way to think of bad online behavior is the use of the Internet to hurt others in some way. Let's explore online etiquette.

Add new guidelines to the poster as you think of them.

TRY THIS!

Begin brainstorming some guidelines for thoughtfully using the Internet on a separate sheet of paper. Work with a friend. Can you think of guidelines for good behavior to keep in mind when online? How about behaviors to avoid? Start with your own thoughts and ideas. Then, as you read this book, go back and add more points to your notes.

Then make a poster. Title it "Online Etiquette." Create two sections on the poster: one called "Dos" and the other called "Don'ts." Fill in each area with points about how you should and shouldn't act online. When you're done, ask a teacher if you can display the poster in your classroom or computer lab.

Chapter Two: Online Etiquette—Your Words

CHAPTER TWO

Online Etiquette—Your Words

Do you have thoughts you don't want others to read? Write them in a journal instead of posting them online.

Cyberspace may seem like a private place. Posting your thoughts online can feel more like writing them in a journal than sharing them with others. You may feel like you can express yourself any way you choose.

When people communicate online, they sometimes forget that their messages reach real people with real feelings. Those messages may simply seem like words on a screen, but keep in mind that your words can be read over and over. Is it possible that what you meant to be funny could be read as hurtful? It can make a big difference when you can't explain your meaning in person. The last thing you want to do is hurt someone's feelings.

Don't be fooled. You are responsible for your actions online. Anything you put on the Internet can be viewed, copied, and used by others. Be thoughtful and careful. Do not post anything that could hurt someone's feelings. Maybe you are writing an e-mail or using a blog

Are you planning to post something online? Think before you type. Ask yourself the following questions:

1. Would I say this to someone's face?
2. Can my message be misread?
3. Would it be better to say my message in person?
4. Would my parents approve if they saw my words?

Did you answer yes to Questions #1 and #4 and no to Questions #2 and #3? Congratulations! There's a good chance you are practicing proper etiquette with your postings.

or wiki. Perhaps you are gaming or designing your own Web site. No matter how you use the Internet, you should practice proper etiquette.

How is talking with someone in person different from writing him an e-mail or chatting online? In person, you can see someone's face. You can hear the tone of his voice. This can help you understand what he means. Online communication is different. It can be difficult to understand the emotions behind someone's words.

TRY THIS!

Try this activity with friends. Everyone should think of a phrase that could be misunderstood in an online posting. Then each person should write it down on a slip of paper. One example is "I can't believe you said that!" Then, everyone should trade papers and read what another person wrote out loud. Read the phrases with different emotions. Try using funny, angry, and excited tones. Do you see how the same message can be understood in different ways? Wording your thoughts carefully is an important part of online etiquette.

Try reading each note in as many different ways as you can.

People sometimes use blogs and wikis to share and discuss ideas. You always want to share information and ideas in respectful ways. You also don't want to share information that could be misleading. Good etiquette also means giving credit to your sources. If you are sharing information you got somewhere else, make sure you cite the source. If you are repeating something that someone told you, make sure you have permission to use the information.

You can visit Web sites created by people all over the globe. What you post online can also be seen by others around the world.

If you don't know whether you need permission to post something, ask a teacher or librarian for help.

Don't be afraid to tell an adult if you see something bad online.

You also want to respect other people's thoughts. Do you disagree with what others have typed in a blog or wiki? You must respect their right to their own opinions. Phrase any comments politely. If someone posts **inappropriate** content, report it to an adult.

Does etiquette also apply to playing games with others online? Absolutely! Gaming can involve friendly competition.

Have you ever been playing an online game when another player started using rude language? He or she was not using etiquette. Don't use a game's chat system to taunt players who lost. If others act inappropriately, leave the game. If others are posting words that seem dangerous, tell an adult. There may be ways to notify the game company of inappropriate behavior. Dangerous words include threats and insults. Remember, online games are meant to be fun!

CHAPTER THREE

Online Etiquette—Your Actions

It is a good idea to ask permission before taking a picture of someone.

We know the importance of choosing words wisely. Now let's think about ways to apply good online etiquette to our actions.

Posting photos to the Internet can be a fun way to share memories with friends and family. You're able to share events that are happening in your life with others whether they are near or far away. Do your grandparents live far away? You can e-mail a photo of your prizewinning science fair project. Any photos you post online should be ones you wouldn't mind everyone seeing.

Etiquette requires us to be considerate in our actions. Posting a picture that could hurt someone's feelings is not responsible. You should also respect the privacy of others. Is there a friend in a photo from your birthday party that you would like to e-mail to a cousin? Ask before sending. Would you want someone to post a picture of you without your permission?

Always consider whether you have permission to use a photo or video clip. Get permission first if you want to post something that is not your property. Cite the source. A teacher can show you the proper way to give credit to your sources.

Embarrassing pictures are no fun for anyone!

TRY THIS!

Do you have friends or relatives who live far away? Keep them updated with some family photos. Make this a family project. Together, think of a way to share your photos online. You could try using a program such as Microsoft Photo Story to create a photo slideshow. Posting photos to a family social network is another option.

Think before posting any pictures or video clips. Could they cause problems for anyone? Are they embarrassing? When in doubt, check with an adult first. Once a picture or video is posted, it can be difficult to control who sees it or passes it on.

Have you ever heard of cyberbullies? A cyberbully is someone who uses the Internet to harass, threaten, or spread rumors. It may seem as if cyberbullies can't hurt anyone because they are just using words, but bullying in any form is dangerous and serious. You want to make sure your actions are never taken as bullying.

Always be careful of what you say and do online. If you aren't, you may be a cyberbully without even realizing it.

Sometimes, people might not even realize they are being cyberbullies. Perhaps you e-mailed an embarrassing photo of a friend to other classmates. Maybe you thought you were being funny, but that behavior is a form of cyberbullying. Your friend would likely feel angry or embarrassed. Remember: If your online actions threaten, hurt, bother, or embarrass another person, you are being a cyberbully.

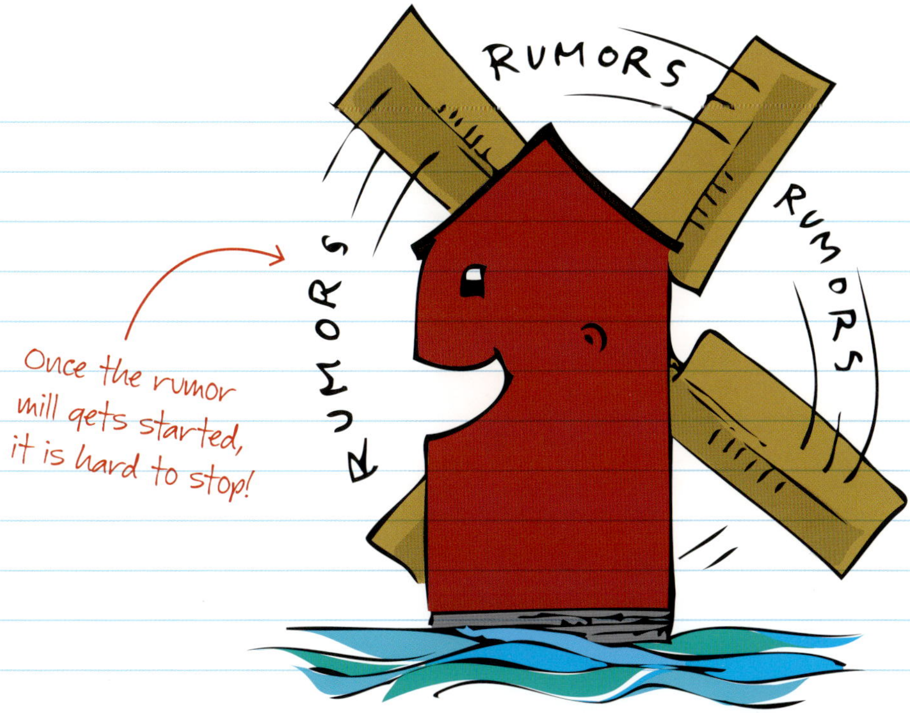

Can you think of a time when someone you know spread a rumor about someone else? Maybe it was something like "Tom doesn't like Ben," or even "Tom hates Ben." Tom didn't really say that. Maybe the person spreading the rumor was upset with Tom. Both Tom and Ben were probably upset by those untrue, unkind words. These kinds of messages can make people feel horrible when they are spread online.

You know you should tell an adult if you see a friend being picked on at school. You should do the same thing when it happens online. We all have the duty of reporting bad online behavior that is targeted at others or ourselves. You may feel embarrassed or afraid to tell someone, but the best way to stop a bully is to tell a responsible adult. Your actions can keep you and others safe.

Here are some tips for dealing with cyberbullies:

- Tell a trusted adult every time someone bullies.
- If you come across a cyberbully at school, let your teacher know.
- Don't open, read, or respond to any sort of message from a cyberbully.
- Don't erase the bully's messages. They may be needed to take action against him.
- Have an adult check to see if the sender of the bullying messages can be blocked.
- Trust your feelings. If something doesn't feel right, it probably isn't. Perhaps someone uses bad language and talks poorly of others in a chat room. Maybe you come across a Web site dedicated to making fun of a classmate. Leave those sites and stay away. Tell an adult.

CHAPTER FOUR

Safety, Part 1

You know the online world is an exciting place to explore. You also know it is important to practice proper online etiquette. It is even more important to keep online safety in mind.

At school, you probably signed an Acceptable Use Policy (AUP). This agreement has safety guidelines for you to follow when using the Internet or electronic resources at school. You don't remember this document?

If you don't follow the rules of your school's AUP, your teachers won't let you use school computers.

Ask your teacher or media specialist to see it. Study the rules you were asked to follow to keep you safe online. It is just as important to set up some online safety rules at home.

TRY THIS!

Talk to your family about creating some Internet safety guidelines. Together, think of safety tips to include. You might want to set the amount of time you can spend online each day. You could state where the computer must be located in your home. Look online for sample AUP contracts for more ideas. Then type up your AUP agreement and print it out. Every family member should sign it. Keep the document near the computer.

While you're at it, why not create an etiquette contract? Type up a list of guidelines for proper online behavior your family will follow. Print it out and have everyone sign this contract, too.

Privacy is an important part of online safety. Online privacy involves keeping your personal information to yourself. Personal information includes your full name, phone number, passwords, and address. It also includes the name of your school and your age.

Never put your personal information online. Don't post any facts or pictures that could allow strangers to find you. Never give out personal information to anyone who asks for it. Some people on the Internet lie about who they are. They may try to trick others into meeting up. Don't trust anyone who is trying to gather your personal information, even if he or she seems nice.

What if you are on a site that asks for information to register? Ask an adult for permission. Use sites that have registration forms that are designed to keep you and your information safe. There are kid-friendly sites that will not collect any information that violates your privacy.

SAFETY FIRST

With your parents, check out kid-friendly sites that ask you to register. One option is Club Penguin (www.clubpenguin.com). What information do they ask for? In what ways are children prevented from giving out their personal information?

Some Web sites have rules that people must agree to follow. Are you on a site that asks you to sign up for an account? Look for that site's Terms of Use and Privacy Policy links. These links may have slightly different names, depending on the site. They are often found at the bottom of the page. The Terms of Use and Privacy Policy can be long documents. Have an adult go through them with you. You need to know what you are agreeing to before you use the site.

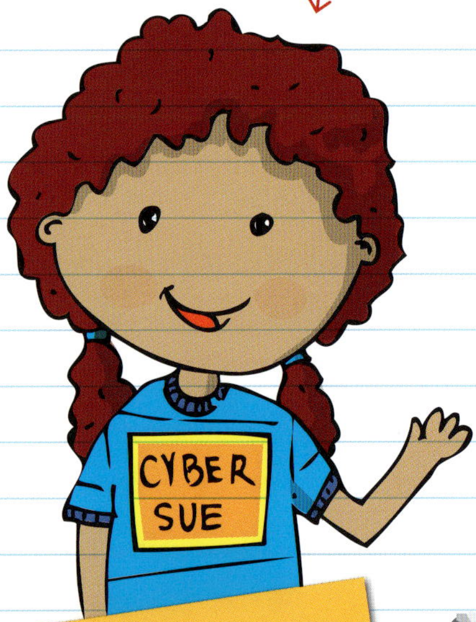

TRY THIS!

Are you visiting Web sites that require you to register? Are you using sites in which others interact with you? Do not use your real name. Instead, make up your screen name or username. You could use your favorite movie or book character's name. You could also think one up. Using a made-up online name can help keep your identity private.

Many sites that require you to sign up for an account are for users ages 13 and older. This is because of the Children's Online Privacy Protection Act. It prohibits Web sites from violating children's privacy. Be careful. Some very popular sites have this rule. You should not get an account until you are more than 13 years of age.

TRY THIS!

Ask an adult to look at some Terms of Use policies of different sites with you. Together, try to find out if there is an age requirement. Here are some options to explore:

- Facebook (www.facebook.com/)
- Voki (www.voki.com/)
- Nick.com (www.nick.com/)
- PBS Kids (pbskids.org/)

Do any of these sites require you to be a certain age to use them?

Always make sure you are old enough to use the sites you visit.

CHAPTER FIVE

Safety, Part 2

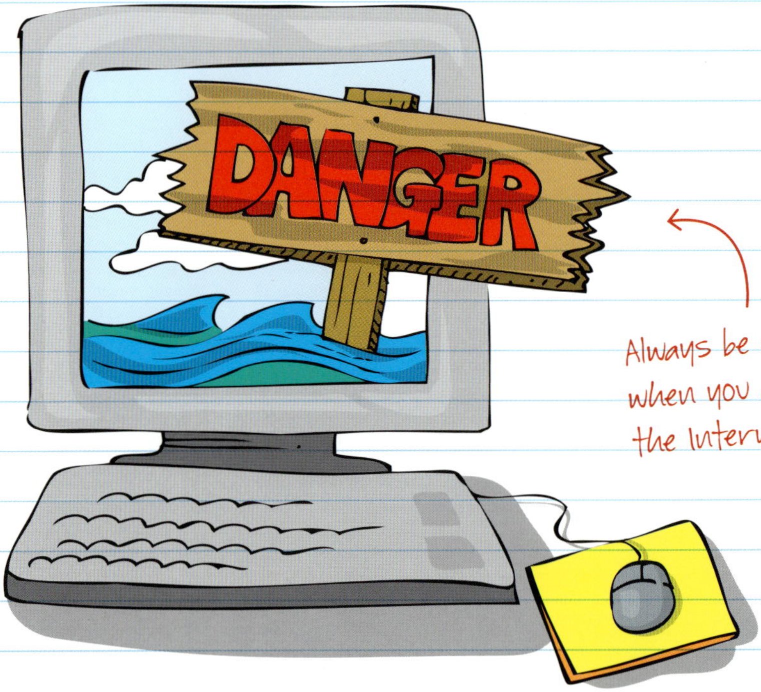

Always be careful when you are using the Internet.

In your day-to-day life, many dangerous places have warning signs. You might spot caution tape at the scene of an accident. You might see "No Swimming" signs along a polluted beach. The Internet is different. You may not find clear signs that say "Stay Away! This Site is Dangerous!" Instead, your common sense and safety smarts will be your warning system when you go online.

Let's say you are using the Internet to gather information for a research project. Your searches may return mixed results. Some sites can be helpful and useful. Some can be inaccurate and misleading. Some may not be for children. Be aware of where the information is coming from.

How do you find safe, useful Web sites? One option is to take advantage of online resources that are available for you to use from your teacher or media specialist. Check out your school or public library. Libraries often provide access to online encyclopedias or databases that are safe and reliable. You could also use kid-friendly search engines. One tool is Yahoo! Kids (*kids.yahoo.com/*).

Your parents might be able to show you some safe, informative Web sites.

TRY THIS!

Go Internet exploring with your family. Your goal? Find some safe informational sites that you can use for help with projects. Then bookmark them for future use. One good place to start is the American Library Association's Great Web Sites for Kids (*www.ala.org/greatsites*). There, you will find safe sites for all age levels and interests.

You can bookmark sites that are safe and useful.

Have you ever been online when some ads suddenly appeared on your monitor? They might have sparkled or flashed and looked exciting. Sometimes, they say things such as "You Are a Winner" or "Click Here." These are pop-up ads. They usually promise you something that is too good to be true. They are often designed to get people to visit an advertiser's Web site. Do not click on pop-ups.

Never click on pop-up ads!

What if a link, advertisement, or pop-up leads you to a site that makes you feel uncomfortable? Close the site immediately or turn off the monitor. Tell an adult. End any online experience right away if it feels inappropriate or dangerous.

Imagine receiving an e-mail. The subject heading promises you something great, but the message is from someone you don't know. Don't be fooled. If something sounds too good to be true, it probably is. Don't open the e-mail. Delete it. Some people send out e-mails to try to get others to send them money. They make up lies that fool people into accepting their offers.

TRY THIS!

Share your online safety smarts with others. Create a brochure about Internet safety. As you work, imagine explaining the safety basics to someone who has never used the Internet before. What points would you cover? Include information about cyberbullies, protecting one's privacy, and other safety topics.

Your word processing software likely has an option for creating brochures. Ask an adult for help if you need it. Then print out enough copies for your class. Fold the brochures and pass them out to your classmates. You should be proud of yourself, Information Explorer. You're spreading the word about the importance of online safety!

Your brochure can help your friends learn about Internet safety.

Chapter Five: Safety, Part 2

If you follow the guidelines in this book, you'll be able to have fun and stay safe online!

It's difficult to imagine life without the Internet. It is such a fun and useful learning tool. Don't forget that you are in charge of your online behavior. Always practice proper online etiquette. Report bad online behavior. Have fun online while being safe and responsible at the same time!

Glossary

blog **(BLAWG)** a Web site that has a personal, online journal with entries from its author

cite **(SITE)** give credit to the source of a fact, quote, or other information

etiquette **(ET-ih-ket)** rules for good or proper behavior

inappropriate **(in-uh-PROH-pree-it)** not right or proper for the situation, time, or place

pop-up ads **(POP-uhp ADZ)** forms of Web advertising that appear in new windows

posting **(POHST-eeng)** publishing or putting work or messages on a wiki, blog, or other online setup

Privacy Policy **(PRYE-vuh-see POL-ih-see)** a statement of how a Web site shares or collects information about visitors

Terms of Use **(TURMZ UHV YOOSS)** a collection of rules for using a Web site and reasons why a visitor's access to a site can be discontinued

wiki **(WI-kee)** a Web site that allows users to add and edit content and information

Find Out More

BOOKS

Bailey, Diane. *Cyber Ethics*. New York: Rosen Central, 2008.

Espeland, Pamela and Elizabeth Verdick. *Dude, That's Rude!: (Get Some Manners)*. Minneapolis: Free Spirit Publishing, 2007.

Jakubiak, David J. *A Smart Kid's Guide to Online Bullying*. New York: PowerKids Press, 2010.

WEB SITES

FEMA for Kids—Online Safety Rules for Kids

www.fema.gov/kids/on_safety.htm

Follow these guidelines when using the Internet.

National Crime Prevention Council—Stay Safe Online

www.mcgruff.org/Advice/online_safety.php

Find online safety tips.

PBS Kids—Get Your Web License

pbskids.org/license/index.html

Answer a series of questions and learn more about safe Internet surfing along the way.

Index

About the Author

Phyllis Cornwall is a media specialist in Michigan. She and her husband, Dr. Bryan Cornwall, love to explore information. Special thanks to Mom, Linda, Lydia, Dan, and Ben for their constant support. Special thanks to her expert students in grades 3–5 who helped her with this book.